CHELSEA'S CUP GLORIES

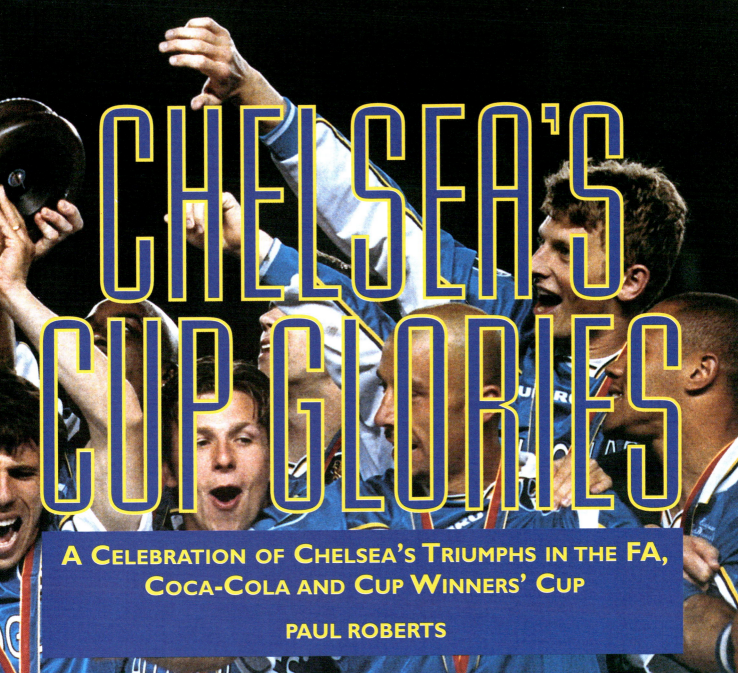

CHELSEA'S CUP GLORIES

A Celebration of Chelsea's Triumphs in the FA, Coca-Cola and Cup Winners' Cup

PAUL ROBERTS

BOXTREE

First published in 1998 by Boxtree, an imprint of Macmillan Publishers Ltd,
25 Eccleston Place, London, SW1W 9NF and Basingstoke

Associated companies throughout the world

ISBN 0 7522 1328 8

Copyright © Paul Roberts

All photographs Action Images

The right of Paul Roberts to be identified as the author of this work has been asserted by him in accordance with the Copyright, Designs and Patents Act 1988.

All rights reserved. No part of this publication may be reproduced, stored in or introduced into a retrieval system, or transmitted, in any form, or by any means (electronic, mechanical, photocopying, recording or otherwise) without the prior written permission of the publisher. Any person who does any unauthorized act in relation to this publication may be liable to criminal prosecution and civil claims for damage.

1 3 5 7 9 8 6 4 2

A CIP catalogue record for this book is available from the British Library

Design and reproduction by Blackjacks, London

Printed in Great Britain by The Bath Press, Bath

This book is sold subject to the condition that it shall not, by way of trade or otherwise, be lent, re-sold, hired out, or otherwise circulated without the publisher's prior consent in any form of binding or cover other than that in which it is published and without a similar condition including this condition being imposed on the subsequent purchaser.

CONTENTS

FA CUP 1996/97 — 6

CUP WINNERS' CUP – BRATISLAVA — 12

COCA-COLA CUP THIRD ROUND – BLACKBURN — 16

CUP WINNERS' CUP – TROMSØ — 18

COCA-COLA CUP FOURTH ROUND – SOUTHAMPTON — 24

COCA-COLA CUP QUARTER-FINAL – IPSWICH — 28

COCA-COLA CUP SEMI-FINAL – ARSENAL — 32

CUP WINNERS' CUP QUARTER-FINAL – REAL BETIS — 38

COCA-COLA CUP FINAL – MIDDLESBROUGH — 42

CUP WINNERS' CUP SEMI-FINAL – VICENZA — 48

CUP WINNERS' CUP FINAL – STUTTGART — 54

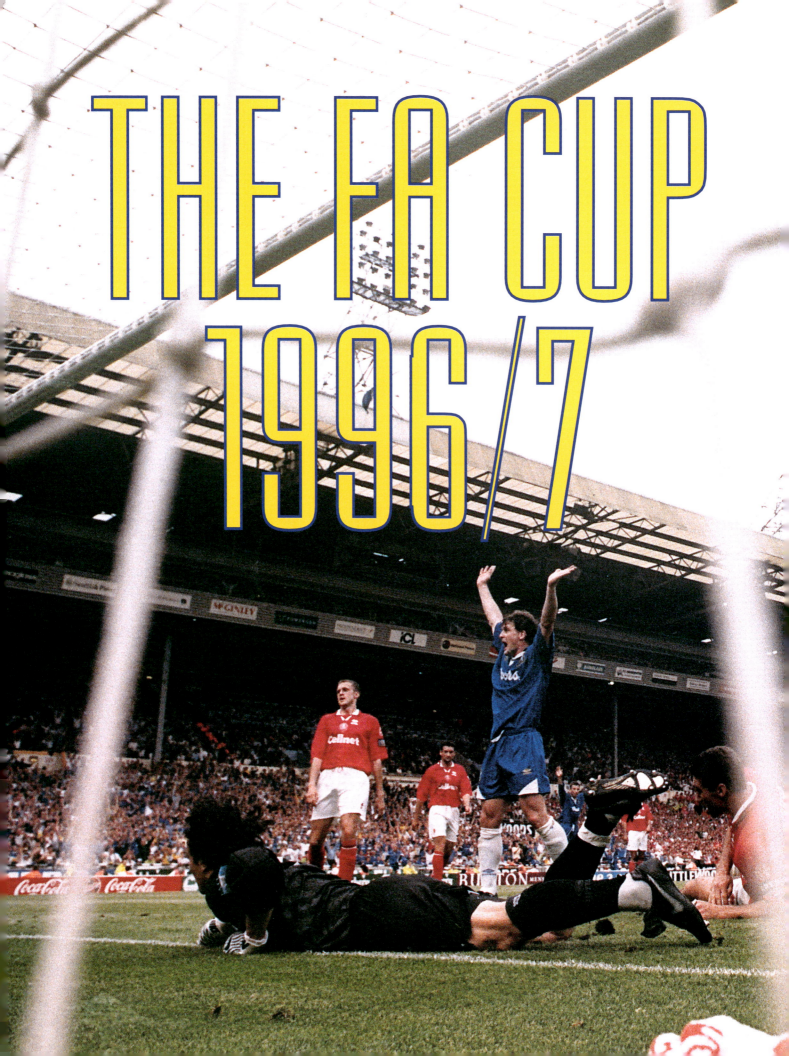

ten minutes before the start of the 1997 FA Cup Final, Steve Clarke turned to his captain Dennis Wise in the Wembley dressing room and said, "This is the day we lay the ghost of the 1970s team. It's about time everyone started talking about us."

The chronic underachievement of the quarter century that had elapsed since Chelsea's triumph in the European Cup Winners' Cup of 1971 had long weighed heavily on the club. While Chelsea had the airs of a big club, other teams got on with the business of winning trophies. It wasn't as if the team had come close to ending that barren run in the intervening years. A shock League Cup final defeat by Stoke City in 1972 heralded the end of the all too short glory years of the seventies and then there was nothing until 1994. Even then the FA Cup Final loss to Manchester United that year will be remembered mainly for being the most one-sided scoreline in Wembley finals.

Three years after that humiliation there was a new belief within the Chelsea camp. World class footballers had been purchased at great expense. Players like Mark Hughes, goalscorer for United in that 1994 mismatch; Dan Petrescu, a Romanian international regarded as the best wing-back in the world; Gianluca Vialli, an Italian legend. Many of the Chelsea squad had won Championship medals with other clubs, throughout Europe. Most were established internationals. These men were accustomed to winning and saw no reason why that should not continue at Chelsea.

For weeks before the May date with Middlesbrough, their attentions, it seemed, had been concentrated on the FA Cup.

Ten minutes and thirty seconds after Clarke had uttered his statement of intent, Roberto Di Matteo collected a short pass from Wise ten yards inside his own half.

The Italian international with the most languid of running styles glided forward effortlessly. As defenders backed off to cover a diagonal run by Mark Hughes, Di Matteo struck the ball with such pace and such precision that it shot straight over the young 'Boro goalkeeper Ben Roberts and then dipped, clipping the crossbar. Three years previously Gavin Peacock's shot had hit exactly the same piece of woodwork only to bounce down and away. With it went Chelsea's best chance of creating an upset. Now, a better player from a better team representing the same club enjoyed greater fortune. As the ball crashed down and then up into the roof of the net, the Chelsea supporters hailed one of the great FA Cup goals. At forty-three seconds, it was the quickest ever recorded at Wembley. The long wait for a trophy was almost over, but for the Chelsea fans in the ground the next 89 minutes would prove to be as much of an endurance test as the previous 26 years.

The run to Wembley had started four months earlier with a home tie with West Bromwich Albion. It was just the sort of fixture that in the past would have unnerved the Chelsea players with the weight of expectation proving too much for them. While the more optimistic supporters pointed out that the only other FA Cup winning team in Chelsea history had claimed the trophy three years after suffering a disappointing final defeat, the players produced a thoroughly professional performance to dispose of the First Division team 3-0. Even though the score was only 1-0 until the final fifteen minutes of the game when substitute Craig Burley and Gianfranco Zola added further strikes, the result was never in doubt. Albion's only effort on goal was a weak header that fell apologetically into the hands of Norwegian goalkeeper Frode Grodås.

Middlesbrough had suffered a wretched season. Backed by the personal fortune of a wealthy chairman, manager Bryan Robson had invested heavily in overseas talent. They were expected to be amongst the frontrunners in the Premiership and by November they were handily placed in the top six. A disastrous mid-season run plunged them into a relegation scrap. The deduction of two points for failing to fulfil a fixture at Blackburn in December because of a severe injury crisis ultimately cost them their place in the top league. Of more concern in the run-up to Wembley was the lack of team spirit within the camp. They became divided between the home-grown artisans and the foreign superstars. Nowhere was this more apparent than during those opening few minutes at Wembley as Chelsea began to control the game.

Chelsea possessed their share of imported talent but unlike 'Boro's collection of individuals, they were a team committed to a common cause. They could have been two ahead within the opening ten minutes as first left-back Scott Minto narrowly failed to convert a half-chance, then Dan Petrescu lifted the ball over Roberts only to see 'Boro

THE FA CUP 1996/97

captain Nigel Pearson clear from under his own bar. For the remainder of the half, Chelsea dominated midfield and never looked in any discomfort. Middlesbrough had the attitude of a team that knew it was beaten in the time it had taken Di Matteo to launch Chelsea into that first-minute lead.

Chelsea had maintained a belief that they could win the 1997 FA Cup even before they had started their first match in the tournament. It was a feeling that was strengthened by an amazing afternoon at Stamford Bridge on the last Sunday in January. Those supporters lucky enough to be present will never forget the Blues dramatic victory over Liverpool.

For the second year in a row, Chelsea had to face the then league leaders in the early round of the Cup. Liverpool and Chelsea were regarded as the best passing sides in the country and whoever won this tie would rightly be regarded as one of the favourites to lift the trophy. The events that unfolded have already been written into the history of Chelsea Football Club.

Ruud Gullit restored Luca Vialli to the starting line-up for the first time in eight games, relegating Mark Hughes, so often a scourge of the Merseysiders, to the substitutes bench. Kevin Hitchcock came in as goalkeeper while in defence Frank Sinclair replaced Michael Duberry from the side that had eased past West Brom in the previous round. For Duberry a freak training ground accident had left him with a ruptured Achilles tendon, ruling him out of the remainder of the season.

Chelsea started poorly and Liverpool were soon into their familiar passing routine. Robbie Fowler and then Stan Collymore, after a loose pass by Zola was miscontrolled by Eddie Newton, gave the Reds a 2-0 lead. But for an inexcusable miss by Steve McManaman, shortly before the break, Chelsea's Cup chances would have been extinguished. Their only chance had been poorly wasted by the out of sorts Vialli.

Gullit had fifteen minutes to make the changes to save his side's season. On came Hughes, at the expense of the left-back Minto. Chelsea went to three at the back, Di Matteo pushed forward to negate the dominance of John Barnes in midfield and Dan Petrescu was given a free role. Up front, Chelsea went for broke as Hughes lined up alongside Vialli with Zola just behind.

Within four minutes of the restart, Hughes, whose physical presence had already begun to unsettle the previously untroubled Liverpool defenders, turned to smash home the first goal. Zola added a second with a magnificent long-range effort. Five more minutes and Vialli had given Chelsea the lead, flicking home a clever pass from Petrescu.

Liverpool were helpless as more chances were created and finally Vialli headed a fourth from a perfect free-kick by Zola. It was almost as amazing a come back for Vialli who had suffered a terrible first half, as it was for the team. The celebrations of the supporters were only slightly dampened when, moments after the final whistle, the draw for the Fifth Round gave Chelsea a difficult away trip to Leicester City.

There was to be no such recovery for Middlesbrough at Wembley. They were forced into two substitutions within the opening twenty minutes. Ravanelli, their expensive Italian import and, so it was said, a source of much of the discord within their camp, limped off with a recurrence of a hamstring injury. He was followed off the pitch moments later by Mustoe, that combative midfielder who might just have made a difference to Chelsea's control of

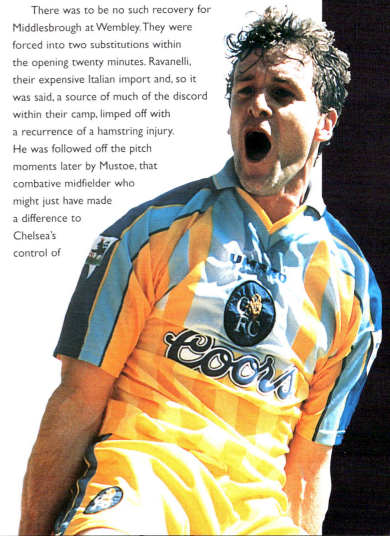

possession. The only occasion that there was the slightest alarm for the Blues came seconds before half-time when Gianluca Festa headed a long cross back across the goal and past Grodås into the net. Even before Festa had made contact, the linesman had raised his flag to nullify the strike. Television replays proved inconclusive. The Italian may have just been level with the last defender but the flag was positive and Chelsea had escaped their one moment of panic. The roars from the Chelsea supporters that greeted the half-time whistle suggested that they were as confident as the team appeared to be.

If an away trip to Filbert Street seemed to be scant reward for the thrilling triumph over Liverpool, then Chelsea appeared to be making light of that supposition. They raced into a two-goal lead at half-time with superb strikes by Di Matteo and Hughes. The first led to cries of 'Italia, Italia!' from the travelling fans. The game was played four days after Chelsea's Italian contingent had starred in their country's World Cup victory over England at Wembley and they had to endure abuse from the home crowd. With Di Matteo's goal, the Chelsea fans showed where their loyalties lay, at least that afternoon.

Leicester, though, are one of the most competitive teams in the league and they came out determined to upset the favourites. They launched a series of high balls into the penalty area and it was from one of these that Steve Walsh halved the lead. It looked as if Chelsea would hold on but with minutes left a free-kick was turned into his own net by Newton. Clarke had been booked for contesting the award of the kick and it did look harsh, but any controversy was overshadowed by what occurred in the replay ten days later.

Chelsea had much the better of the second game and created a number of chances. The Leicester 'keeper Kasey Keller was in outstanding form to deny Di Matteo, Zola and Vialli while his opposite number Grodås had little to do. Even so, Leicester nearly grabbed an undeserved win when Leboeuf was forced to clear off his own line in the final minute of normal time.

With extra-time ticking away and Leicester's ambition of taking the tie to penalty kicks within sight, substitute Erland Johnsen made one last run forward, only to stumble under pressure from a defender. Contact, if any, was minimal, but the referee pointed to the spot. The ice-cool Leboeuf stroked home the kick and two nerve racking minutes later, Chelsea were in the last eight.

The outcry over the award of the referee's decision was unprecedented. There were calls for the game to be replayed and the referee involved, Mike Reed, was universally condemned for his decision. He was even withdrawn from officiating in the upcoming league fixture between the two teams. What the complainants forget though, is that Chelsea totally dominated the game and deserved to win. Little was made of the unfair decision that had led to Leicester's equaliser in the first game and if the limit of a team's ambition is to win a game on penalty kicks then they cannot complain if their luck does not hold out.

Chelsea needed no such piece of luck at Wembley. While Middlesbrough found the occasion too much, the Blues were totally assured and appeared to be enjoying the surroundings. Dennis Wise dictated possession, Di Matteo was his usual assured elegance. Petrescu created space with ease along the right flank and Eddie Newton, on the few occasions he had to, gave his defence excellent cover. Frank Leboeuf and Steve Clarke were solid at the back and the full-backs Minto and Sinclair seemed to spend more time going forward than in defence. Hughes dominated his markers and Zola, despite clearly not having fully recovered from the hamstring strain that had at one stage threatened to keep him out of the Final, was always dangerous. For goalkeeper Grodås, it was one of the easiest afternoons of his short Chelsea career.

As comfortable indeed, as the quarter-final tie at Portsmouth. The First Division team had shocked Leeds United at Elland Road in the previous round. They felt that they could intimidate the foreigners in the Chelsea line-up with overly physical play which, sadly, all too often went unpunished by some weak refereeing. What they forgot though, is that Mark Hughes revels in that sort of treatment. His brilliant volley gave Chelsea the lead in the first quarter and they were always in complete control. Further goals from Wise, a rare double for the captain, and Zola saw Chelsea through to their second consecutive semi-final.

Gianfranco Zola had been named as the Football Writers' Footballer of the Year in the week preceding the final, thereby becoming the first Chelsea player to win the prestigious

award. He had enjoyed an astonishing season in England, even more remarkable for the fact that he had not arrived in this country until November. Despite suffering a hamstring injury shortly after the semi-final, great things were expected of Franco at Wembley. He often threatened the spectacular but it never quite worked for him, a venomous free-kick and a mazy dribble that ended with a shot from a narrow angle well saved by the 'Boro keeper, apart.

There was nothing to compete with his wonder goal in the semi-final victory over Wimbledon. Half-way through the second half, with Chelsea ahead through a Mark Hughes tap-in moments before half-time, Franco received the ball on the edge of the penalty area with his back to goal. In one move, he touched the ball back across goal, turned his defender and powered the ball into the corner of the net. In one magical moment Zola had destroyed the morale of a Wimbledon team that was almost universally expected to upset Chelsea. The team that had launched an aerial blitz to win at Stamford Bridge earlier in the season could make no impression on the Norwegian rocks of Johnsen and Grodås.

Zola was expected to perform similar miracles in the Final. There was nothing quite as spectacular but his contribution, when it came, was brilliant and important. As the clock ran down Chelsea were content to keep possession and wait for the time to strike. They had kept the ball for fully 60 seconds when Newton made a break forward and passed to Petrescu on the edge of the area.

Petrescu's cross appeared to have too much weight on it but Zola, skilfully, leapt high to flick it back into the danger area where Newton forced home to register his first goal of the season.

After 26 years and 82 minutes of waiting, the Chelsea supporters could celebrate the capture of a major trophy.

The celebrations were the longest and loudest Wembley has ever known. Almost three decades of frustrations were purged as the team became the first to perform two laps of honour around the famous old stadium. It was fully 45 minutes after the final whistle before they could drag themselves away from the ecstatic masses. Those that doubt Chelsea Football Club is of any importance to the local community should have witnessed the celebrations that continued around Stamford Bridge until the early hours. Yet even as the traditional open-top bus parade made its way to Fulham Town Hall the following morning, thoughts turned to Europe and the question of whether this team could be good enough to emulate Chelsea's only other FA Cup-winning team and capture a European trophy.

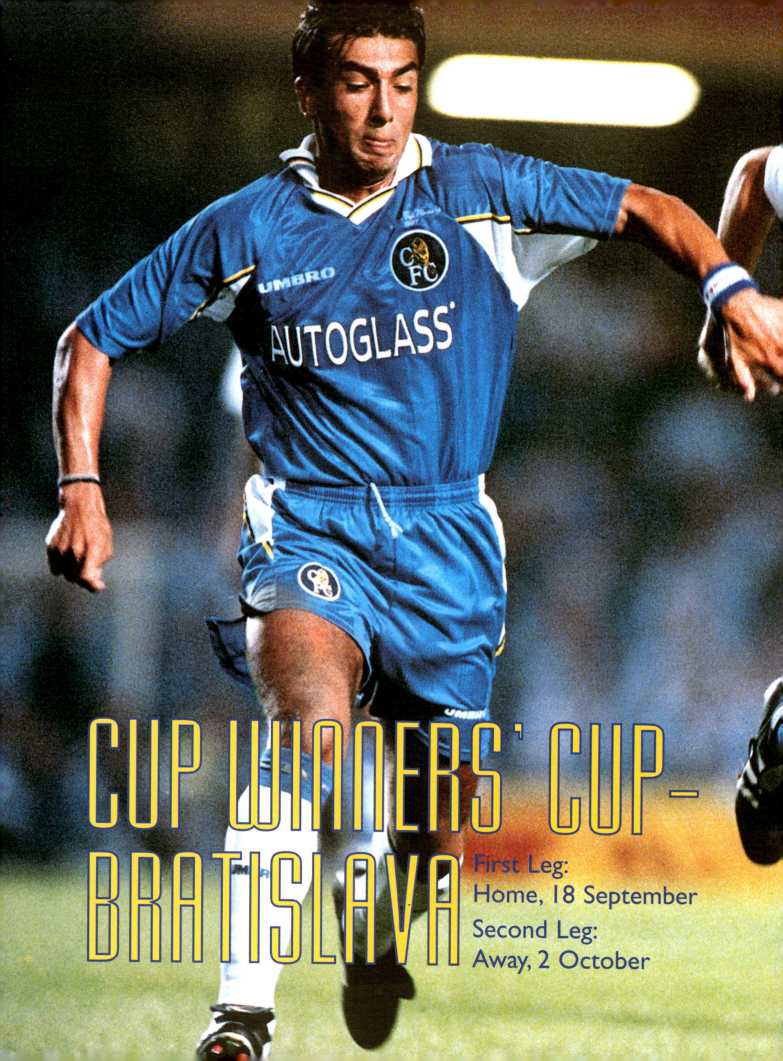

CUP WINNERS' CUP – BRATISLAVA

First Leg: Home, 18 September
Second Leg: Away, 2 October

Chelsea had reached the semi-finals of the European Cup Winners' Cup in 1995. On that occasion, they were considered impostors. Runners-up to Manchester United in the FA Cup Final, they only qualified for the competition as United, fortunately for Chelsea, also won the league. The fact that they reached the last four, while battling against relegation for much of the domestic season, was hailed as a triumph. This time around, Ruud Gullit's expensively assembled cast of superstars was installed as favourite to win the trophy almost as soon as Dennis Wise collected the FA Cup.

Three internationals had already been signed even before the game against Middlesbrough. Celestine Babayaro, Tore Andre Flo and Gustavo Poyet were soon joined by goalkeeper Ed de Goey from Dutch football; Bernard Lambourde came from France, and then on the very eve of the new campaign a club record £5m was spent on bringing Graeme Le Saux back to Stamford Bridge from Blackburn. For Le Saux, the contrast between the club he had left four and a half years previously and the new Chelsea could not have been greater. Then, Chelsea had just sacked Ian

Porterfield and were diving headlong towards another relegation battle. Now European football beckoned and there was a strong belief amongst the team that a genuine challenge for the Premiership title could be mounted.

There were other reasons for the optimism, at least with regards to Europe. The change in the format for the Champions League to allow the runners-up in the richest domestic leagues to join that competition meant that the holders Barcelona were absent. Also, several entrants from those countries that traditionally supply the majority of European champions were not the most famous of clubs. Even at that early stage, the two strongest challenges to Chelsea's chances were felt to be the Germans Stuttgart and Real Betis from Spain. So it proved.

Even so, there were a few inward groans when the draw for the First Round, held the day before Stamford Bridge hosted a match for the first time in the season, paired Chelsea with Slovan Bratislava. It wasn't that the team wasn't confident about progressing but as a seeded team, the draw could have been much kinder to Chelsea. Slovan were undoubtedly the most dangerous of the unseeded teams. While Stuttgart travelled to Iceland, Chelsea had to take on the only other previous winners of the Cup Winners' Cup in this season's field. The team from Slovakia, who had won through a tough Preliminary Round tie against Lokomotiv Sofia, proved to be a shadow of their famous predecessors who had famously upset Barcelona in the 1969 final.

By the time of the first leg, confidence was soaring among the Chelsea team. A run of four consecutive wins with fifteen goals scored had taken the team to third place in the league and already ten different players had found their way onto the goalscoring lists.

Manager Ruud Gullit had to contend with problems of selection for the first leg with both regular full-backs Frank Sinclair and Graeme Le Saux suspended. Sinclair had been booked during the second-leg of the semi-final against Real Zaragoza in 1995 to earn a suspension and had waited over two years to serve it. Le Saux was still serving the ban he had received for striking his Blackburn team-mate David Batty during a Champions' League tie in Moscow in 1996. Paul Hughes was drafted in as an emergency right-back and Danny Granville came in on the left. Gianluca Vialli partnered Gianfranco Zola in attack as Gullit relied on Vialli's immense experience in Europe. Luca is one of a select group to have won all three European trophies.

At least Gullit did not have to deal with the controversial rule that stated only three non-nationals could appear for a club in Europe. Three years ago that rule had caused untold disruption to the Chelsea team as Glenn Hoddle had to shuffle his team depending on which 'foreigners' were to be included. With the rule banished as a by-product of the Bosman ruling, Chelsea fielded just four Englishmen against Bratislava.

It was an Italian, Roberto Di Matteo who opened the scoring with a low shot across the goalkeeper in the 12th minute. The slightly disappointing crowd of 23,000 settled back and waited for the goals to flow, but that just didn't happen. Vialli and Zola struck the woodwork but Di Matteo's goal was the only one of the first half and the tension was beginning to show around the ground.

The second half followed the pattern of the first. Chelsea pressed but were unable to create a clear chance. At least Bratislava showed no likelihood of snatching a vital away goal. Finally, with just ten minutes remaining the young defender Granville ventured forward into the opposition penalty area. As Paul Hughes hit a hopeful cross, Granville showed considerable composure to control the ball, lift it over a stranded defender and hit home the second goal to give Chelsea a comfortable lead for the second leg.

During the two weeks before they flew out to Bratislava, Chelsea had played tough games against three of the teams considered to be rivals for the league title, Arsenal, Manchester United and Newcastle United. A last minute defeat by Arsenal was frustrating enough, but perhaps of more important consequence was a nasty ankle injury to Michael Duberry that would keep him out of action for eight weeks.

For the second leg at the bleak Tehelne Pole stadium Bernard Lambourde was moved from midfield to partner Frank Leboeuf, while both Sinclair and Le Saux returned to the side in Slovakia. On a heavy pitch, the team struggled to settle into their passing game and it took a giant slice of luck to ease the nerves. The goalkeeper Miroslav Konig tried to clear a back pass but his clearance struck Luca Vialli on the thigh and rebounded off the crossbar and down inches behind the goal-line. The referee's assistant signalled the goal and Chelsea could relax.

With the away goal, Bratislava needed four goals and in that position, Gullit brought on Celestine Babayaro to make his Chelsea debut. Di Matteo added a second and from then on the most difficult opponent to deal with was the swirling wind. It wasn't the last time that Chelsea had to deal with extreme weather conditions during their European adventures.

With what looked like an easy tie against the Norwegian team Tromsø in the next round, Chelsea could return to domestic action and plan their assault on the Coca-Cola Cup.

CUP WINNERS' CUP – BRATISLAVA

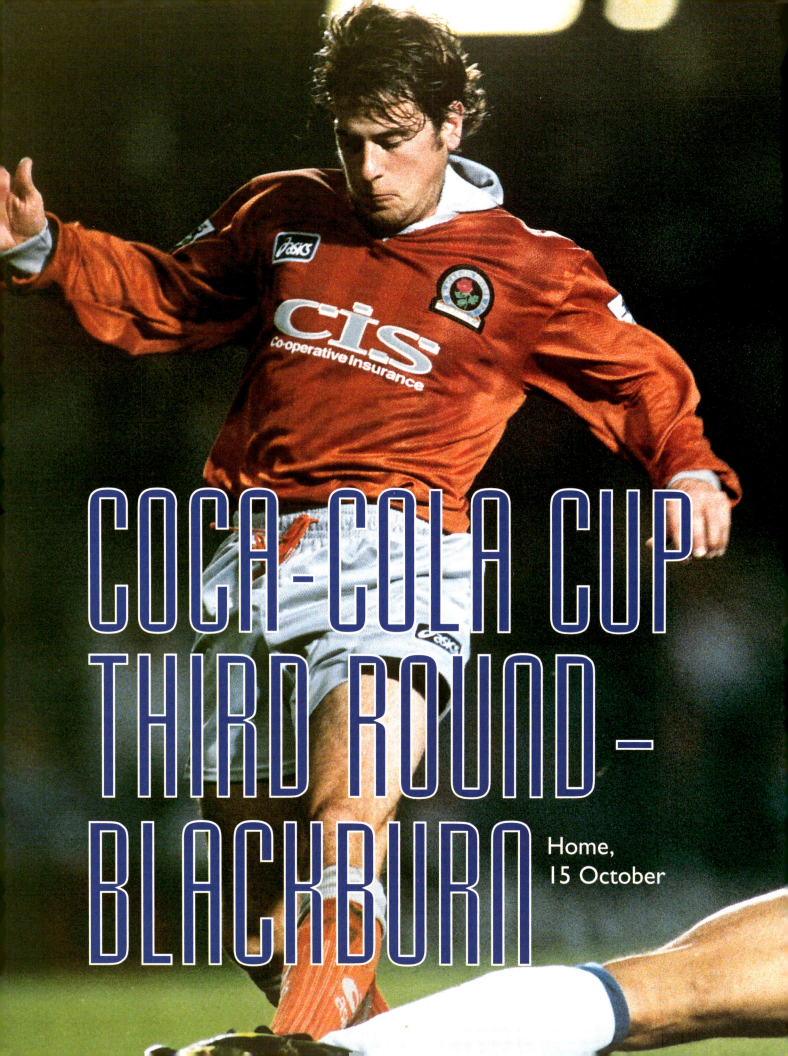

COCA-COLA CUP THIRD ROUND – BLACKBURN

Home, 15 October

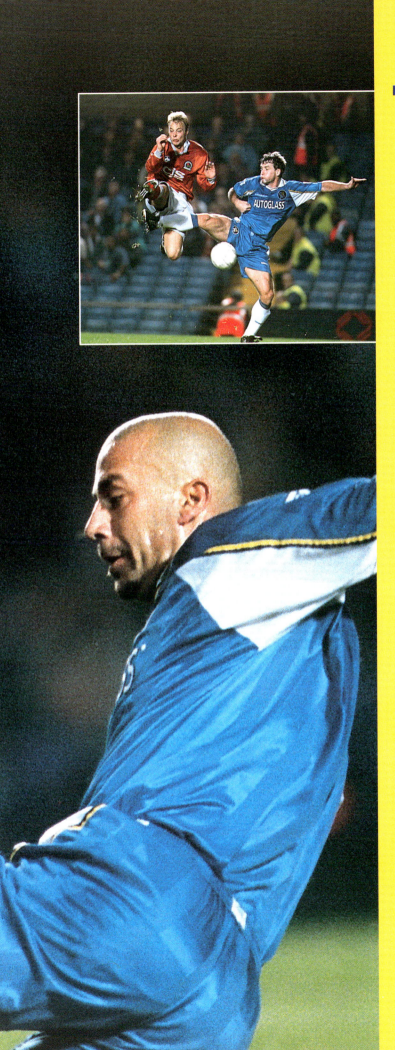

The tie against Blackburn came in the middle of a busy period for the team. The only occasions that Chelsea had not had a midweek fixture had been international weeks. With so many players featuring in those games, Gullit decided to rest several of the stars for what he considered to be the least important competition of the four in which Chelsea were entered. At this stage of the season, there was to be no European qualification for the winners of the Coca-Cola Cup and several top clubs took the opportunity to rest key players. Chelsea were to be the only side with sufficient quality in depth to justify that policy.

Kevin Hitchcock came in as goalkeeper, Gullit played alongside Leboeuf and Mark Nicholls and Granville also started. Steven Hampshire was named amongst the substitutes and he came on to make his first-team debut two days before his 18th birthday. Another substitute, David Lee, made his first appearance after a broken leg had kept him out for almost a full year. It was a clear indication of where the priorities lay against a team that fielded a full strength side.

Chelsea are yet to defeat Blackburn Rovers in a Premiership game, but that poor record was not apparent in the early stages as the team set about their opponents. Vialli, in particular, seemed keen to take advantage of a rare appearance at Stamford Bridge and he came closest to opening the scoring in the first half.

When Billy McKinlay scored after a Leboeuf error at the start of the second half, Chelsea's only crowd of less than 20,000 for the whole season, feared the worst. Then Leboeuf atoned for his mistake by setting up Di Matteo for a fine equaliser.

Even though Vialli was sent off for striking Henchoz under the gaze of the assistant referee, the team held on comfortably during extra-time to take the tie into a penalty shoot-out.

Kevin Hitchcock has a fine reputation for winning penalty shoot-outs and so it proved again. He saved from Sutton and saw Bohinen blaze over. Leboeuf, Sinclair and Clarke were all spot-on and then Mark Nicholls dispatched the final kick past England goalkeeper Tim Flowers to settle the match. Having been exempt from the Second Round of the Coca-Cola Cup because of their involvement in Europe, Chelsea now found themselves in the last sixteen of the competition. With some top clubs already eliminated they were widely fancied to go all the way.

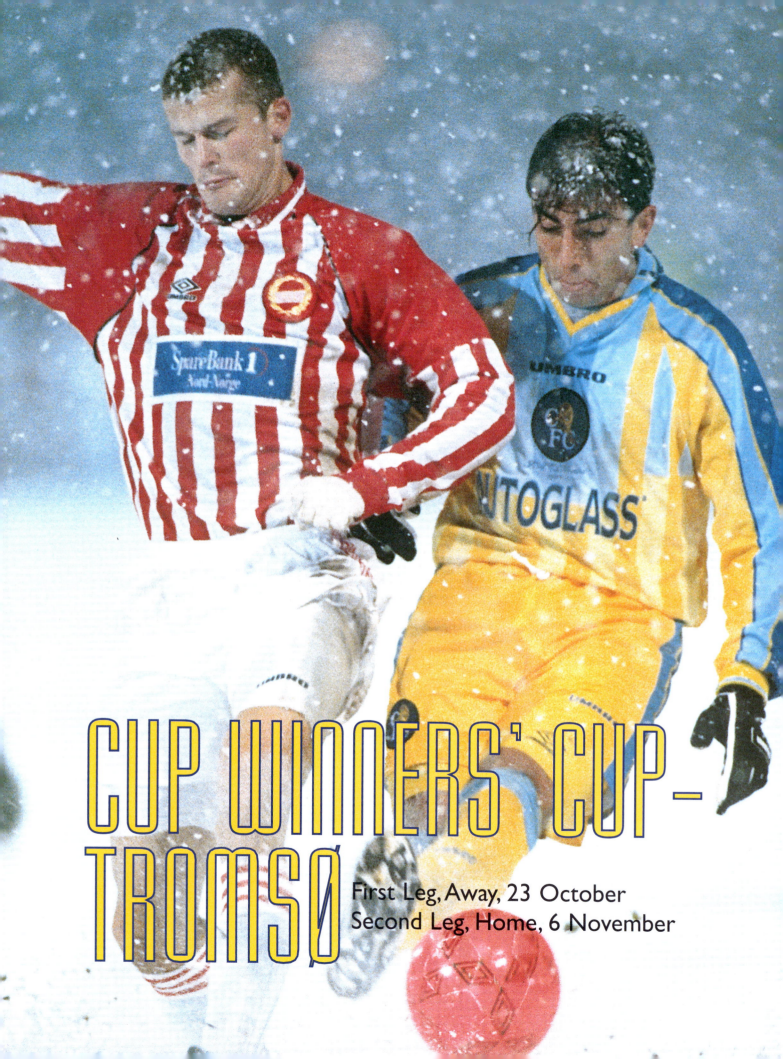

CUP WINNERS' CUP – TROMSØ

First Leg, Away, 23 October
Second Leg, Home, 6 November

the tie against Tromsø should have been a formality for Chelsea. The part-timers had won the Norwegian cup competition for only the second time in their history, but that game had been played the previous October at the end of the summer season. In the meanwhile, they had lost several of their star players. Despite a promising start to the current campaign, they had plummeted towards the relegation zone. Their final league fixture resulted in a 4-0 defeat at already relegated Lyn Oslo to leave them facing a play-off to retain their status in the Norwegian Premier League. As it transpired the standard of the opposition was not the greatest threat to Chelsea's passage into the quarter-finals.

Tromsø is a beautiful town, situated on an island off the northern Norwegian coast, linked to the mainland by one suspension bridge. It also lies 210 miles within the Arctic Circle and by late October, when the first leg was due to be played, the severe winter conditions had begun to arrive. It was suggested after the draw was made that the fixture would be moved to the capital Oslo, but Tromsø insisted that

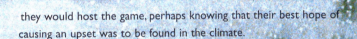

they would host the game, perhaps knowing that their best hope of causing an upset was to be found in the climate.

The chartered airplane carrying the Chelsea team touched down at the tiny Tromsø airport thirty hours before kick-off. On the day of the game there was bright sunshine until darkness fell at 4pm. Shortly before the team was due to leave their hotel, a sudden blizzard fell from the skies covering the pitch with snow. Even though the snowfall had occurred so late in the day, the intensity of it meant that there had to be serious doubts as to whether the game could go ahead. The snow eased though and the covers that had lain across the pitch for several days were removed to reveal a pudding of a pitch, with soft mud across the centre and dangerously hard, rutted turf in the corners.

In those circumstances it was something of a surprise to the 500 or so loyal Chelsea supporters who had made the long journey that when the teams were announced Gianluca Vialli and Gianfranco Zola were paired in attack, even though many felt that the conditions were more suited to the heavyweights Mark Hughes and Tore Andre Flo, a former Tromsø player.

Chelsea were soon in trouble as they failed to deal with either the pitch or their opponents. Within five minutes a needless free-kick was given away and Steinar Nilsen, playing in his last few fixtures for the club before moving to AC Milan, struck home from twenty yards to give Tromsø the lead. The Norwegians gained heart from this and continued to press, their basic long-ball tactics causing problems for the Chelsea defence. In return, the Blues tried to maintain their normal passing game, but time and again they lost possession as passes went astray on the difficult surface.

Tromsø looked dangerous whenever they had the ball and it was no surprise when they extended their lead. Eddie Newton and Dennis Wise lost possession and Frode Fermann took advantage. He was under no pressure as he advanced to the edge of the area and shot in off Ed de Goey's shoulder. It was a bad mistake by the big goalkeeper who looked uncomfortable all night, not just because he had decided not to wear tracksuit bottoms in favour of shorts only. If it was a brave statement of intent aimed at the Tromsø forwards, then it didn't work.

Thankfully, Chelsea made it to half-time only two goals behind. Mark Hughes replaced the left-back Granville as Gullit gambled everything on snatching a vital away goal. Chelsea's formation wasn't

CUP WINNERS' CUP – TROMSØ

21

all that changed during the interval. The snow returned with a vengeance, covering the pitch. The wind blew the snowstorm directly towards the goal Chelsea defended after the break and many of the team later complained that their eyes hurt so much that they had difficulty even seeing the ball. Twice the referee called a halt to the proceedings so that the groundstaff could brush the snow from the various lines around the pitch. On both occasions Gullit leapt to his feet imploring the officials to abandon the game. He discovered later that the referee was under pressure from the UEFA delegate to finish the game that evening at all costs.

Five minutes from the end Gianluca Vialli, who had played poorly throughout the game, collected a long pass and turned his marker. An attempted pass to Zola was deflected back to Vialli and he deposited the ball past Tor Andre Grenersen. It was the away goal that Chelsea desperately needed but barely deserved. Even then, there was more drama to come. As Vialli celebrated the goal, Frank Leboeuf limped to the half-way line. He had been suffering from a hamstring injury for some minutes and couldn't continue. Replacement Andy Myers was refused permission to come on and Tromsø kicked off.

They launched a long ball forward and Ole Martin Årst found himself in the position that would have been occupied by Myers. With a free shot at goal he couldn't miss. Now Myers was allowed on but Chelsea were again two goals down.

At least they now had the away goal, and deep into the time added on for 'snow breaks' they conjured another goal. Myers, under instructions simply to fire the ball long did just that. Hughes managed to touch on a header and there was Vialli again, turning inside his marker, then outside, inside once more and firing home across the keeper. At 3-2 down, Chelsea had escaped with a result that made them favourites to advance into the last eight when they could so easily have found themselves all but out.

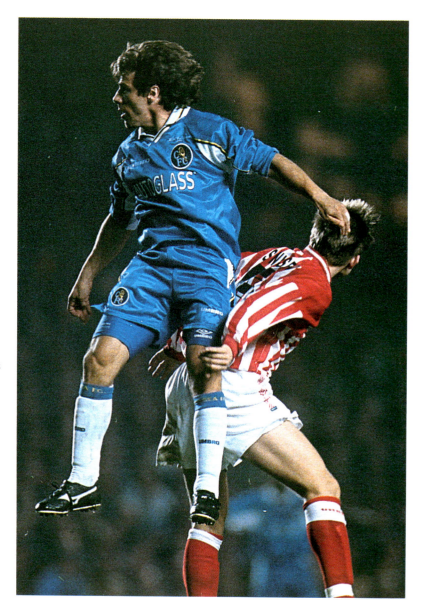

CUP WINNERS' CUP – TROMSØ

The team stayed in Tromsø overnight before returning home. Two days later a tired team went down limply at Bolton Wanderers new stadium despite dominating possession. A win at Aston Villa a week later kept them in fourth place, and in good heart for the return with Tromsø. The Norwegians for their part had won the first leg of their relegation play-off 4-0 against EIK Tonsberg. A few eyebrows were raised at Stamford Bridge when it was discovered that the game, which took place just three days after Chelsea's visit, had been moved indoors as their regular pitch was deemed unplayable.

The Chelsea players were determined to win the second game comfortably. They had been stung by comments, in Norway and in England, that they were lucky in the first game. They knew that they had not played well but were anxious to prove, on a decent surface, the class between the two sides. Myers started alongside Leboeuf, Petrescu returned to midfield and Vialli again partnered Zola.

The result was never in doubt from the moment Petrescu headed home in the 12th minute. Vialli added a second and although Bjorn Johansen pulled one back, a Zola free-kick, only his second dead-ball goal for Chelsea, made the game safe before the interval. Further goals from Leboeuf, a penalty, Vialli, who completed a hat-trick, and Petrescu in the final five minutes emphasised the true gulf between the two teams. A potentially difficult tie had been safely accomplished. Now Chelsea had to wait five weeks for the quarter-final draw to be held. With the next round not scheduled until March, thoughts could return to the Coca-Cola Cup.

COCA-COLA CUP FOURTH ROUND – SOUTHAMPTON

Home, 19 November

Chelsea went into the Fourth Round tie against Southampton buoyed by a win over West Ham United, the first time they had won the league game following a European fixture. Again, Ruud Gullit made changes. If anything, it was an even weaker team than had taken on Blackburn. Hitchcock returned in goal, Gullit named himself in defence, regular reserves Granville, Morris, Nicholls and Lambourde also came in. Perhaps most significantly, 19-year-old Nick Crittenden made his first team debut.

The difference in experience between the two teams was apparent early on. David Hirst clipped the crossbar when perhaps he should have scored and Hitchcock was called into action on several occasions. Gullit had a poor game in defence. No doubt his mind was on more important matters,

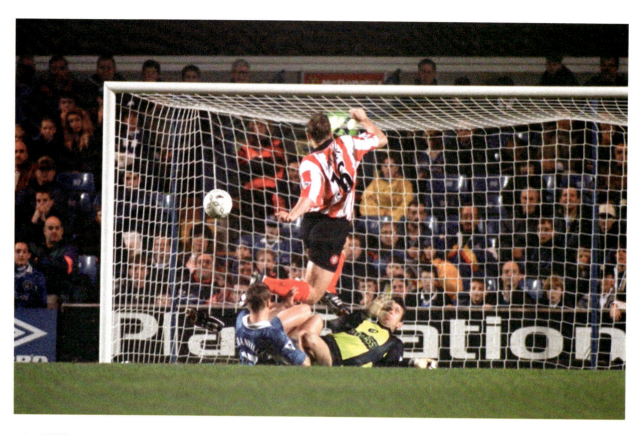

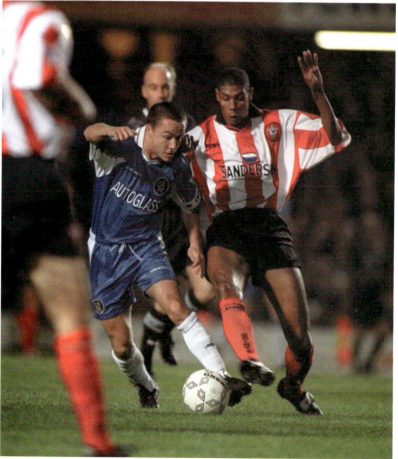

his baby daughter being born a day before the game. Chelsea badly missed the composure of Leboeuf and always looked vulnerable to the pace of Hirst and Kevin Davies.

Southampton took the lead early in the second half. A loose pass by Gullit was collected by Matthew Le Tissier who set Davies away. The young forward just got to the ball before Hitchcock and slipped the ball in off the far post. The visitors twice had good chances to score again but were thwarted by the stand-in Hitchcock who proved yet again that he is the country's most reliable reserve goalkeeper. Still, they looked comfortable until Chelsea fashioned a spectacular equaliser. There appeared no danger as Tore Andre Flo collected a pass from young debutant Nick Crittenden on the right touch line. In an instant the Norwegian had turned past Francis Benali and Claus Lundekvam, and unleashed a powerful shot inside Paul Jones' near-post. It was a brilliant way for Flo to register his first goal at Stamford Bridge.

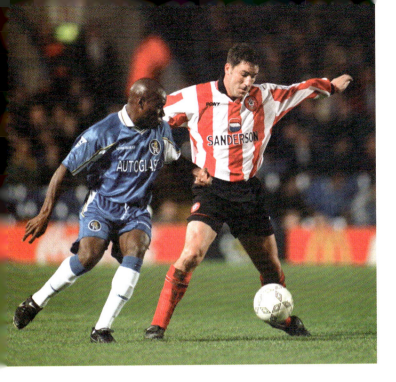

the tournament, he controlled the ball on the edge of the area and nudged it back for Jody Morris to curl a right foot shot into the top corner. It was a goal worthy of winning a cup tie but even then Chelsea had to endure an anxious moment as with almost the last piece of action in the game, Le Tissier directed a weak header into the grateful arms of Hitchcock when he really should have scored. Chelsea's youngsters held on and the club had reached the last eight of a major cup competition for the eighth time in seven seasons.

A crowd of almost 21,000, a surprisingly large attendance given that the game was televised live, had been greatly entertained. Chelsea had fourteen shots on target during the game, more than any other match to that point of the season. Southampton's tally was ten. Chelsea forced 21 corners, an unbelievable amount. Against a team that had won five of its previous six matches, it was an encouraging performance.

The two goals opened up play and either team could have won in normal time, but thirty more minutes were required to separate the sides. At half-time in the extra period, Mark Hughes replaced Dennis Wise. It was Hughes' physical presence that was to win the tie for Chelsea. With just three minutes remaining before Chelsea's second penalty contest of

For too long, Chelsea had made little impact in this competition. Now, having reached the last eight by means of a penalty shoot-out and a late winner, there was a genuine belief amongst the team that with a favourable draw they could go all the way. Being paired with First Division side Ipswich Town in the quarter-finals merely served to strengthen that belief.

COCA-COLA CUP 4TH ROUND – SOUTHAMPTON

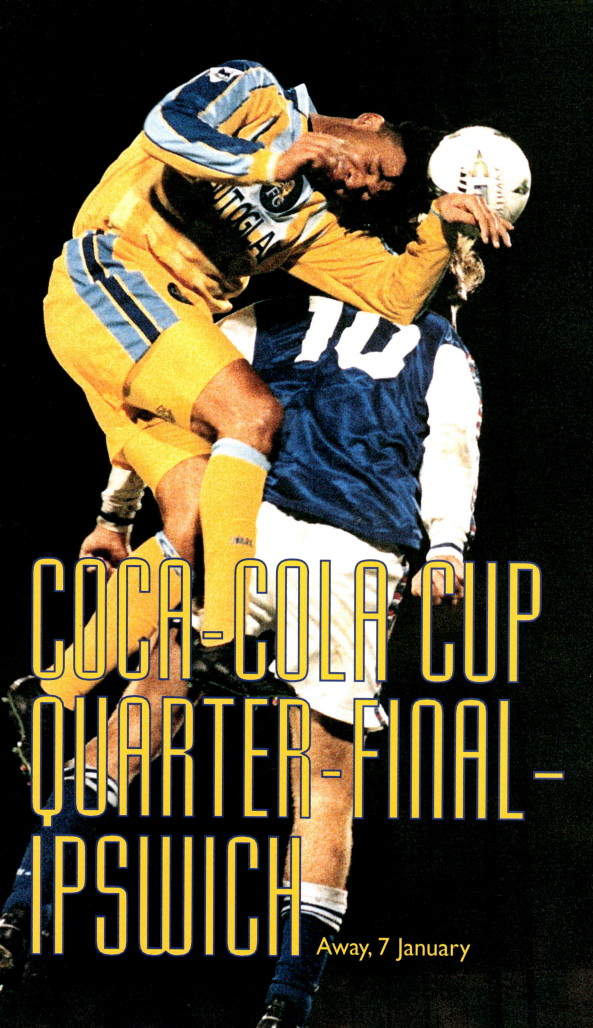

COCA-COLA CUP QUARTER-FINAL – IPSWICH

Away, 7 January

With the hectic schedule of the first three months of the season now completed, Chelsea could concentrate on their Premiership campaign. A run of eight consecutive league games, the longest of the entire season, was scheduled before Chelsea were due to open their defence of the FA Cup. It was during this period that Chelsea arguably played the best football of their season. Big wins over Derby County, Tottenham Hotspur and Sheffield Wednesday moved the Blues into third place in the Premiership, and although disappointing home draws against nine man Leeds United and Wimbledon gave the first indications that they would not be able to sustain a challenge on that front, they were still confident going into the FA Cup Third Round clash against Manchester United.

That optimism was misplaced. United destroyed Chelsea. The final score of 5-3 was misleading as Chelsea had netted three times in the final fifteen minutes with the game already lost. It was a credit to the players that they were able to finish strongly but the gulf between the two sides was greater than the scoreline suggested. How ironic then that Chelsea would finish the season with two trophies and United none.

After such a blow, it was important that Chelsea regained some confidence with a victory. Just three days later they faced Ipswich Town at Portman Road in the quarter-finals of the Coca-Cola Cup. Suddenly, this tournament assumed new significance. Out of the FA Cup, seven points behind the league leaders and with the next round of European competition not scheduled for a further eight weeks, the players could concentrate on this trophy.

Another factor was the news that the Football League were now optimistic that the winners of the tournament would be allowed to participate in the following season's UEFA Cup. No decision was to be made until after the quarter-finals but it gave the game an added edge. While some of the clubs already knocked out may have questioned the justice of changing the rules during a competition, it certainly heightened the expectancy amongst the eight clubs still left in.

Ruud Gullit made six changes from the side that had beaten Southampton in the previous round. In came de Goey, Leboeuf, Di Matteo,

Le Saux and Zola, in a clear indication that Chelsea were now taking the tournament very seriously indeed. Still, the effects of a flu bug that was sweeping Stamford Bridge and the after-effects of the FA Cup tie three days earlier were apparent in the opening moments of the game. The Chelsea midfield struggled to contain an Ipswich team enjoying a good run in the league and it took a mistake from the home goalkeeper Richard Wright to present Chelsea with the lead. Wright had no chance of intercepting a through ball and as he came rushing out of his area, Le Saux lifted the ball over the stranded keeper for Flo to head into an unguarded net.

Shortly before half-time, magnificent interplay between Gullit, Flo and Zola carved open the home defence for Le Saux to add a second. It should have been comfortable from then on but a failing of Chelsea's had been the loss of concentration after scoring, especially just before the interval. So it proved again as the home side capitalised on some indecisive defending and Mauricio Taricco bundled the ball home barely a minute after Le Saux's goal.

This gave the home side a new surge of enthusiasm they might not otherwise have had and they dominated the second half as Chelsea tired. It was no surprise when they equalised, Alex Mathie shooting home after substitute Gullit had lost possession. Ipswich finished the stronger and Chelsea were grateful to hear the referee's whistle to signal the end of normal time. It gave the weary players a much needed chance to regroup.

Both teams had chances in extra-time, Zola volleying over and Bobby Petta hitting the post for the home side in the dying minutes when it appeared inevitable that he would score. On such margins are trophies won and lost. For the second time in the Coca-Cola Cup, Chelsea faced a penalty shoot-out and this time Ed de Goey was the hero, saving twice, from Taricco and James Scowcroft, before Mark Hughes powered home the decisive spot kick. Even before the players left the pitch they received the news that they would face London rivals Arsenal in the two-legged semi-final.

COCA-COLA CUP QUARTER FINAL – IPSWICH

COCA-COLA CUP SEMI-FINAL ARSENAL

First Leg, Away, 28 January
Second Leg, Home, 18 February

team selection for the first leg of the semi-final at Highbury was complicated for both Chelsea and Arsenal by the fact that the game coincided with an international week. Roberto Di Matteo was required by Italy, while Frank Leboeuf and Patrick Vieira of Arsenal were both selected by France. Ironically, Leboeuf was to appear for France only as a last minute substitute for his country and Vieira did not play at all. The absences affected Chelsea more, especially as captain Dennis Wise was also missing with a troublesome toe. Ruud Gullit selected himself to play in place of Leboeuf, Newton partnered Lambourde in the centre of midfield and Flo and Zola were the preferred forward combination.

Chelsea struggled to contain Arsenal in any part of the pitch. The only surprise was that it took Arsenal as long as 22 minutes to open the scoring. A chip over the defence was misjudged by Gullit and the ball bounced off the top of his head into the path of Overmars who slipped the ball under his compatriot de Goey. Arsenal dominated the first half and changes had to be made.

At half-time, Laurent Charvet came on for his debut in place of Frank Sinclair as Chelsea switched to a back three. Within a minute of the restart, with Charvet still getting used to his new surroundings, Arsenal attacked down the left and the cross was converted by Steven Hughes. At that time, it looked as if Chelsea would be lucky to escape with a three-goal deficit to make up in the second leg. Bergkamp could have secured that three-goal lead but his fierce volley was brilliantly saved by de Goey. It was the defining moment of the semi-final. Within sixty seconds Chelsea were on the attack and Zola's cross was deflected onto the head of substitute Mark Hughes, who steered it past the out-of-position Manninger. Instead of being three behind, Chelsea had secured a vital away goal. At 2-1 down, the situation was far better.

Even so, the team had to ride its luck in the remaining 25 minutes as Arsenal continued to press. The final whistle brought mixed emotions amongst the players. It had been a wretched performance, the only saving grace being that they had given themselves at least a chance of progressing in the second leg. After the game, Ruud Gullit spoke confidently to the press about Chelsea's prospects.

At that stage, no-one could have envisaged the events that would overtake the club before the second game.

On Thursday 12th February, four days after another dismal defeat at Highbury, this time in the league, a press release from Chelsea announced that Ruud Gullit was to be replaced as manager by Gianluca Vialli with immediate effect. The news came as a complete surprise to everyone in the game, not least the Chelsea supporters, many of whom gathered outside Stamford Bridge to digest the astonishing developments. At a hastily convened press conference at the ground that afternoon, the club stated that Gullit had asked for too much money when negotiating a new contract – his current deal was due to expire in June – and that the difference between the two parties was too great. In those circumstances it was felt that if negotiations continued it would have an unsettling effect on the players, the backroom staff and the club as a whole.

For his part, Gullit clearly believed that there was more to it than a merely financial question. At another press conference,

COCA-COLA CUP SEMI-FINAL – ARSENAL

35

organised by Gullit's agent the following morning, a visibly upset Gullit demanded to know the real reason for his departure. Further statements put out by the club suggested that Gullit had begun to feel the strain, he was spending too much time away from the training ground and was becoming too involved in personal marketing matters to concentrate on the main business of managing Chelsea. Although Chelsea had won the FA Cup in Gullit's first season, were placed second in the Premiership and were still in two cup competitions when he left, they felt it was time for a change.

It was a difficult situation for Gianluca Vialli to walk into. At least he would have no problems in trying to motivate his first team. The incentive of reaching Wembley would do that for him.

For his first match as manager, the second leg of the Coca-Cola Cup semi-final against Arsenal, Vialli bravely went with a three-man attack of Hughes, Zola and himself. Three midfielders, Petrescu, Di Matteo and Wise, were asked to do the work of four. It was a gamble, but it worked in spectacular fashion. Arsenal were hindered by the absence of internationals Seaman, Keown, Bould and Wright, while Bergkamp and Parlour were clearly less than fully fit. Surprisingly, Arsenal left Hughes, scorer of three goals in the two recent games between the sides, on the bench. They sorely missed his competitiveness in midfield as Chelsea ripped into their opponents.

They were ahead inside ten minutes as cup tie specialist Mark Hughes spun to lash a loose ball into the corner of the net. It gave Chelsea the confidence they needed against the country's in-form team. They dominated possession for the remainder of the first period, confident in the knowledge that should they not concede a goal then a place in the final was theirs.

The key moment in the second leg came three minutes after the restart. Le Saux was crudely hacked down by Vieira. It was the Frenchman's second booking of the game and he was sent off. Within two minutes, as Arsenal struggled to reorganise themselves, Di Matteo took possession within the centre circle, ran towards goal and unleashed an unstoppable shot into the very top corner of the net. It was an amazing goal, better even than his Wembley strike nine months earlier.

Two minutes later Petrescu controlled a half-cleared corner and sweetly hit home the third. A strangely subdued Arsenal side never really threatened to score the two goals needed to take the tie into extra time. Even a Bergkamp penalty with ten minutes remaining, after Duberry had handled while lying on the ground, failed to ignite any true belief in the visitors. They knew that they had been well beaten by a better team.

Chelsea were back at Wembley and how Stamford Bridge celebrated. Gianluca Vialli had become surely the first manager in football history to lead his side to a major final in his first game in charge. It had been a brilliant performance against the odds by Chelsea against a team that was enjoying a great run of success. Twenty minutes after leaving the pitch, Vialli and his new charges discovered that their Wembley opponents would be Middlesbrough, surprising victors over Liverpool in the other semi. It was to be a repeat of last season's memorable FA Cup Final.

CUP WINNERS' CUP QUARTER-FINAL – REAL BETIS

First Leg, Away, 5 March
First Leg, Home, 19 March

after the emotional highs of the victory over Arsenal, the team found it difficult to maintain their challenge in the league. Successive defeats by Leicester City and Manchester United, both without scoring a goal, had all but destroyed their chances of lifting the trophy that was after all, the main priority of the season. The European competition became the number one target.

Prior to the quarter-final draw, Chelsea had been one of the eight seeded teams which helped to account for the relatively easy passage into the latter stages of the competition. Now it was a free draw and the fates were not kind to Chelsea, pairing them with the one other outstanding side left in, the Spanish team Real Betis. Betis did not have a famous pedigree; this was only their fifth European campaign and the first time they had reached the last eight. In fact, they had not even won the Spanish Cup, being runners-up to Barcelona. Yet they were beginning to reap the benefit of investment by their wealthy chairman and had emerged from the shadows to become a major power. It would have been the most difficult of prospects for an experienced manager, let alone one facing only his fourth game in charge.

For the first time, Vialli dropped himself from the starting line-up, preferring Tore Andre Flo in attack with Gianfranco Zola and Dan Petrescu just behind in support. Duberry was given the role of marking Betis' dangerous lone attacker Alfonso, while Clarke and Sinclair were asked to take care of the wide attackers Robert Jarni and Finidi George. The game plan worked to perfection on a balmy Mediterranean evening.

De Goey had just one save to make in the opening few minutes, comfortably gathering an Alfonso shot low down to his right. Within seconds, he turned defence into attack and a clever pass by Di Matteo turned the home defence and set up Flo. The Norwegian beat Olias, moved outside the sweeper Hristo Vidakovic and powered home a shot across the keeper into the far corner. The north-east terrace erupted as over 4,000 Chelsea fans, many of whom had been forced by the local police to enter the ground fully two hours before kick-off and wait without refreshments, hailed what could prove to be a crucial away goal.

Four minutes later, those supporters had forgotten the hardships of that long wait. A Betis attack foundered on a typically robust Steve Clarke challenge. The ball broke to Petrescu who fed Flo. With one goal already to his name Flo had the confidence to skip around his marker and slide the ball under Prats in the Betis goal. Less than twelve minutes played and already Chelsea were two up. The home crowd was silent and their players bemused. What was supposed to be a cagey night of European football was threatening to become a rout.

It took Real Betis fully thirty minutes to recover from the shock. Although they forced a number of corners, dangerously played in by the otherwise disappointing Jarni,

they never seriously threatened de Goey's goal. Indeed, Chelsea could have settled the tie within the first 45 minutes. Moments before the interval, they broke and Zola found himself inside the penalty area only to be pushed over from behind. Astonishingly, the Bulgarian referee awarded a free-kick to Betis and booked the unfortunate Zola for diving. The referee had been a late replacement for the original official, a Swede who had been recognised on television enjoying the hospitality of the Betis chairman at a recent Spanish league game. Perhaps Ouzounov did not want to be accused of favouring the visitors.

Having looked so comfortable in the first half, disaster struck Chelsea right at the start of the second. Within 60 seconds Betis had pulled a goal back, Alfonso heading home after the Chelsea defence had failed to take advantage of several chances to clear the ball. If the home supporters felt that their team would go on to win at least the home leg, they were mistaken. The expected siege of the Chelsea goal never happened. Betis did produce a series of crosses but these were comfortably dealt with by the outstanding Duberry and Leboeuf.

The only difficult save de Goey had to make was from a header by Alfonso in the very last minute. Indeed, had not a Dan Petrescu goal been wrongly ruled out for offside or had not Mark Hughes miskicked while clear on goal in the final few minutes, then Chelsea's advantage would have been even greater. As it was the 2-1 scoreline was to be one of the best away performances by any English team in Europe in recent years. It meant that Betis had to win and score at least twice on a ground where Chelsea had never lost in European competition.

If the first game against Betis had been one of Chelsea's most assured performances in recent seasons, then the return was full of apprehension, at least during the opening 45 minutes. Vialli had made seven changes from the team that

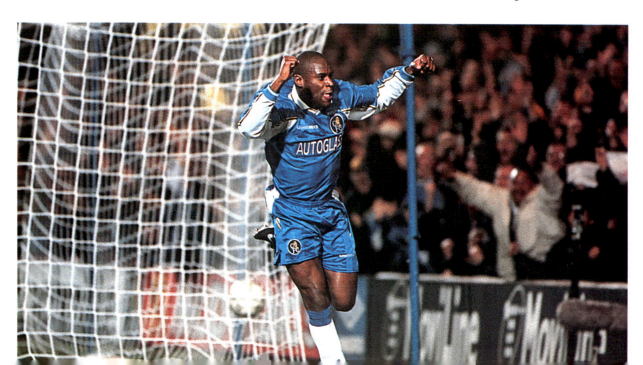

had lost the previous league game at West Ham. De Goey returned in goal to replace Dmitri Kharine and Steve Clarke came in at left back. Despite the success in the first leg, the two full-backs, Clarke and Sinclair, were asked to mark the opposite wingers than they had in Spain. The lack of cohesion in defence was apparent in the very first minute when Leboeuf fouled Alfonso and de Goey was forced into a brilliant save to turn over a savage free-kick by Jarni.

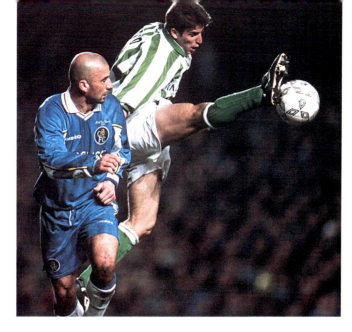

Betis continued to press and they deservedly took the lead on the night when the Nigerian Finidi George ran between Clarke and Leboeuf to latch onto a flicked pass by Alfonso and shoot low past de Goey. The aggregate scores were now level and even though Chelsea still led by virtue of that second away goal, Betis looked more likely winners. It was vital that the Blues established a grip on the game. Just nine minutes after falling behind they were level. The inexperienced Josete fouled Vialli wide on Chelsea's right and from Zola's free-kick Frank Sinclair escaped the attentions of Josete to head home. It was a vital goal by the newly capped Jamaican international.

Fortunate that Chelsea were still ahead on aggregate at half-time, Vialli and Graham Rix were able to make the changes that would win them the tie. The midfield had been overrun for long spells in the first half. The flat midfield quartet switched to a diamond shape with Dennis Wise pushed forward to counter the dangerous Alexis who was dominating the game. The Betis coach, Luis Aragones, a man with a history of impassioned outbursts against Spanish footballing authorities was in no position to counter these moves by Chelsea. He had been sent off at half-time by the German referee after accusing him of home bias. Although Aragones later emerged amongst his team's supporters behind the dug-outs, he was soon led away by stewards.

Within four minutes of the restart, the changes had had a profound effect on the game. Di Matteo robbed Marquez and while the Spaniards complained that his foot had been raised too high, the Italian with a flair for scoring goals on big occasions cut inside the sweeper and hit a cool shot across Prats into the far corner.

Chelsea were in control now, but it could have been an anxious few minutes if Oli had not had a goal ruled out, wrongly as the television replays were to prove later. As it was, the home supporters could not fully relax until substitute Lambourde and Vialli had combined to set up Zola for the third, a crisp shot from the edge of the area.

Zola had suffered a poor run of form and had not scored since November before netting twice against Crystal Palace a week earlier. It was a welcome return to form for the popular Sardinian. A 5-2 win against a top quality Spanish side was an impressive victory and set up the team for the return against Middlesbrough. With Aston Villa and Manchester United losing in their respective European competitions, Chelsea were left on their own to represent England. Not for the last time this season, the supporters let everyone know that there was only 'One Team in Europe!'

For the players, there was little time to savour the victory over Betis. The Coca-Cola Cup Final was to be the next game and thoughts turned to Wembley.

CUP WINNERS' CUP QUARTER-FINAL – REAL BETIS

COCA-COLA CUP FINAL – MIDDLESBROUGH

Wembley, 29 March

After the tribulations of relegation, Middlesbrough had recovered well and were well placed to regain their place in the Premiership at the first time of asking. The signing of new players had revitalised their team and after beating Liverpool in the semi-final, they were extremely confident of gaining revenge for their FA Cup Final defeat by Chelsea. The optimism was misplaced. What Middlesbrough had forgotten was that Chelsea were a better team, with better players more accustomed to the big game atmosphere.

Eight of the Chelsea team had featured in the first final between the two. The three newcomers had all strengthened the team. De Goey was now established in goal, Duberry played in his first final, while record signing Le Saux had recovered sufficiently from the ankle injury that had kept him out since before the first game against Real Betis to come in at left-back for the unlucky Clarke. Hughes and Zola again played in attack as Vialli left himself out. With just three substitutes named, the manager could not even find a place for himself on the bench.

There was a different attitude amongst the two teams. Middlesbrough were determined to win their first ever major trophy but for Chelsea the occasion was more about clinching that all-important place in the next season's UEFA Cup regardless of their final league position.

As the two teams walked out onto the pitch to an explosion of noise, the Chelsea supporters teased the opposition fans with a chant of 'We're going to score in a minute,' a reference to Roberto Di Matteo's record-breaking strike in the FA Cup Final. It took a little longer than that this time around but the final outcome was in as little doubt as it had been ten months earlier.

Middlesbrough settled quickly and Merson caused the rusty Le Saux some awkward moments in the early stages but that threat was soon snuffed out as Di Matteo moved over to help out defensively. Hughes, playing in his eleventh major final, forced an outstanding save from Schwarzer with a brilliant volley and then mistimed a header when it appeared easier to score. Petrescu and Di Matteo launched shots that flew narrowly wide as Chelsea dominated the first period without making the vital breakthrough.

The pattern of play continued after the break. Zola unleashed another powerful shot that beat Schwarzer only to bounce back off the bar, and Di Matteo was inches wide from

COCA-COLA CUP FINAL – MIDDLESBROUGH

the rebound. Middlesbrough's only two chances came half-way through the second half when long passes from midfield caught out the Chelsea rearguard but the sluggish Hamilton Ricard was unable to capitalise as Sinclair used his pace to cover from full-back.

Much of the pre-match conjecture was whether 'Boro's most recent signing, the errant genius Paul Gascoigne, would start the game. As it was he came on as substitute for the ineffective Ricard but was unable to change the flow of Chelsea's attacks. It was Chelsea's own substitute Tore Andre Flo who had the greater influence on the game. After eighty minutes of dealing with the combative Hughes, Middlesbrough's defenders now had a different style of opponent with which to contend. Flo's quick feet and trickery with the ball turned the 'Boro defence and forced their midfielders backwards. Chelsea were much the stronger team but the failure to make the breakthrough caused some anxiety amongst the support. One piece of misfortune late on could give Middlesbrough a win that they would not deserve.

As normal time ended, both teams knew that they were only thirty minutes away from yet another penalty shoot-out. Middlesbrough seemed resigned to the fact that this was the most likely way that they would lift the trophy, while Chelsea were determined to make their superiority tell before then.

The impressive Dennis Wise began to dominate the centre of the pitch and it was his cross, after a breakdown between Middlesbrough's England internationals Gascoigne and Merson, that gave Sinclair a simple header to open the scoring four minutes into extra time. Wise's performance in such an important game again made a complete mockery of the England manager Glenn Hoddle's decision to continually ignore him for international honours. The Chelsea captain earned one of the biggest cheers of the afternoon when he nutmegged Gascoigne in the dying minutes of the contest, if contest it was by then. Earlier in the match Gascoigne had brought down Wise when he was running through on goal. It was a foul that would have surely led to a card if it had been perpetrated by anyone else but the already booked Gascoigne.

Flo continued to torture the Middlesbrough central defenders for the final fifteen minutes of the game and it was from his clever run and shot that Chelsea won the corner from which they clinched the game. Zola mishit the corner kick past the slipping Mustoe and Di Matteo was on hand to sidefoot his customary goal against Middlesbrough. Chelsea could have scored more, Di Matteo missing a simple chance after another thrilling Flo run but it was very

comfortable. The defence had restricted their opponents to just one shot on target for the second time in a final.

It was the first time that the club had won this trophy at Wembley and Wise generously allowed Luca Vialli the honour of leading his team up the famous steps and collecting the cup. It was a proud moment for the man who had won a trophy for his team in only his ninth game in charge.

For the second time in ten months, Chelsea had lifted a trophy at Wembley and again the celebrations were long, loud and exuberant. Chelsea's only previous victory in this competition came way back in 1965, when it was still known as the League Cup, before the final was played at Wembley and it came to be regarded as one of football's major prizes. Having waited so long to win a trophy, the players and supporters were enjoying the taste of victory and wanted more. With a place in the last four of the European Cup Winners' Cup already assured, the sights were turned to that prestigious tournament.

COCA-COLA CUP FINAL – MIDDLESBROUGH

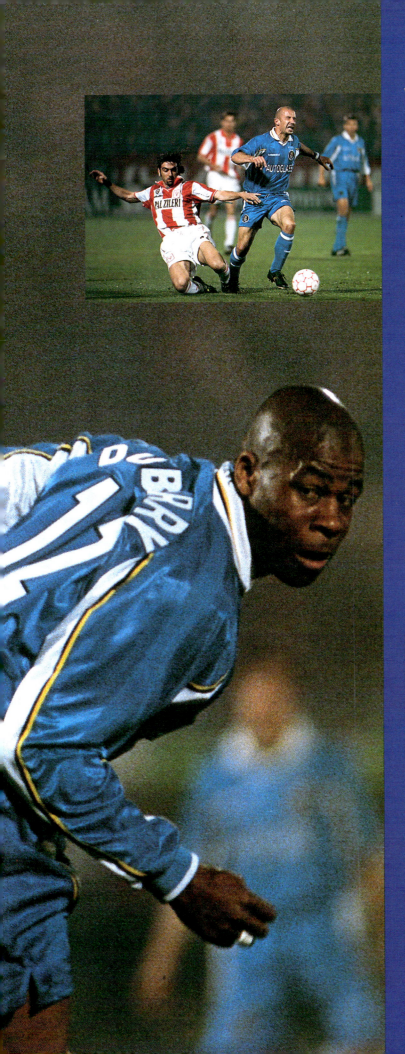

Whether it was the energy-draining exertions of the Wembley victory, or the fact that Vialli had selected the wrong tactics, the performance against Vicenza was an immense disappointment, one that threatened Chelsea's very existence in the competition. Vialli played himself as a lone attacker with Zola in support but he was isolated for much of the game.

In addition, the mental pressure was beginning to tell as much as the physical. This was the third consecutive game that Chelsea had played in cup competitions; the quarter-final against Betis, the Coca-Cola Cup Final and now a European semi-final. Perhaps it was no surprise that this was a very tired performance even against a team that was playing in a European competition for only the second time and could not be considered as one of the best Italian teams.

Chelsea's negative approach handed the initiative to Vicenza. De Goey had already made an outstanding save from a free header after a corner before the home side took the lead in the 15th minute. Lamberto Zauli beat Eddie Newton to the ball and as de Goey advanced the striker mishit the ball past the keeper and in off the far post.

Now Chelsea were caught in two minds. Conceding such an early goal meant that they were unsure whether to chase the game, trying for that vital away goal and risking going further behind, or to sit back and hope to contain the home side.

They kept the score down to one owing to another inspired display by Ed de Goey. The tall Dutch international had an unsteady start to his career in England but he had performed heroics during Chelsea's two cup runs. The stretching save he made to keep out Pasquale Luiso's shot midway through the second half was one of the best made by a Chelsea goalkeeper in recent seasons.

Chelsea did have some chances, particularly after Flo had replaced Petrescu to play down the right flank. Zola hit the post with a cross-shot, Leboeuf had a header cleared off the line and Vicenza received a lucky break when their keeper Pierluigi Brivio sliced a clearance between the waiting Flo and Vialli.

In truth, Chelsea could consider themselves fortunate to escape with just a one-goal deficit to make up in the second game. Without an away goal and without Di Matteo, who collected his second booking of the tournament, Chelsea were the outsiders to make it through to the final. Certainly

CUP WINNERS' CUP SEMI-FINAL – VICENZA

the Vicenza players and supporters celebrated as if they had already clinched their place in Stockholm.

If the performance in the first leg was unsteady, then that in the second was one of the best ever by any Chelsea team. It was considered that the Blues would only retain any chance of progressing if they managed to keep a clean sheet, something of a rarity during the league campaign, at Stamford Bridge. In the absence of Di Matteo, they were cheered by the return of Gustavo Poyet who would make his first start since rupturing knee ligaments in October. Le Saux also returned with Sinclair still out, Zola and Vialli had the responsibility of scoring the goals to take Chelsea through.

Both sides had early chances. Vialli powered a header straight at Brivio who also did well to save low down at his near post from Zola. Vicenza though, were not content to sit back on their lead and went looking for the away goal from

the first whistle. De Goey saved well at the feet of Marco Schenardi and kept out a deflected shot from Ambrosetti.

After half an hour disaster struck as Vicenza scored. It was a farcical goal. Duberry's poor clearance was collected by Zauli who easily beat Newton and scooped the ball over Leboeuf, who was looking to play offside, not knowing that Le Saux and Clarke were out of position. Two attackers nearly collided before Luiso lifted the ball over de Goey and into the far corner. Chelsea had created little in two hours of play against the Italian side and now had to score three times in sixty minutes. It was a time for heroes to emerge.

Three minutes after that potentially decisive strike, Chelsea were level. Le Saux's cross was cleared to Zola who shot low and hard. Brivio parried the shot and

Poyet hooked in the rebound. It was a great piece of skill by the man who had been out injured for so long and the goal gave Chelsea heart. Then, in the final seconds of the first half, Chelsea twice survived moments of panic. First, Luiso had a goal ruled out for a marginal offside decision and then Leboeuf cleared off the line after the same player had slipped the ball over de Goey.

Half-time came and Chelsea knew that they had to score twice more. It was still an enormous task but after five minutes of the restart, Vialli collected a loose ball and powered down the right wing. His cross was perfect for Zola to launch himself at the ball and crash home his first headed goal for the club. The powerful header flew within inches of Brivio but such was the pace of the ball that the goalkeeper stood no chance of reaching it. One goal needed now and for ten minutes the Vicenza defence creaked but it did not crack. They seemed to have played their way out of trouble and Chelsea were running out of time and out of ideas.

In desperation, the old warrior Mark Hughes was sent on to play alongside Vialli and Zola. It was all or nothing now. Just five minutes after making his bow, Hughes got his head to a long clearance from de Goey and as the ball dropped out of the night, he volleyed it past Brivio. It was a goal only Hughes could have scored and Stamford Bridge exploded with celebration.

Suddenly, Vicenza had to chase the game. Even after Massimo Ambrosini was sent off with two minutes left on the clock, they pressed forward. Deep into injury time they launched one last, desperate attack. Arturo Di Napoli brushed past Clarke and put in a dangerous cross to the far post. As Marcelo Otero flung himself at the ball, de Goey used the full length of his long arms to get down and get the merest of touches to the ball. It was a vital intervention and it won the game for Chelsea.

As Andy Myers ran the ball out of the danger area the referee sounded the final whistle. Two of Chelsea's biggest heroes on a night of fourteen heroes, de Goey and Poyet embraced in the penalty area while a third, Mark Hughes, lay prostrate on the turf, the victim of an elbow to the head by an unsporting opponent. Chelsea were through to their second European final, their third in any competition in less than twelve months. It was a remarkable achievement by a club that had underperformed for too long.

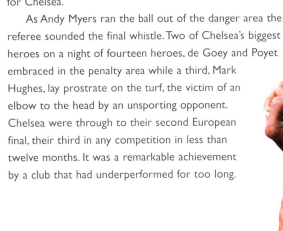

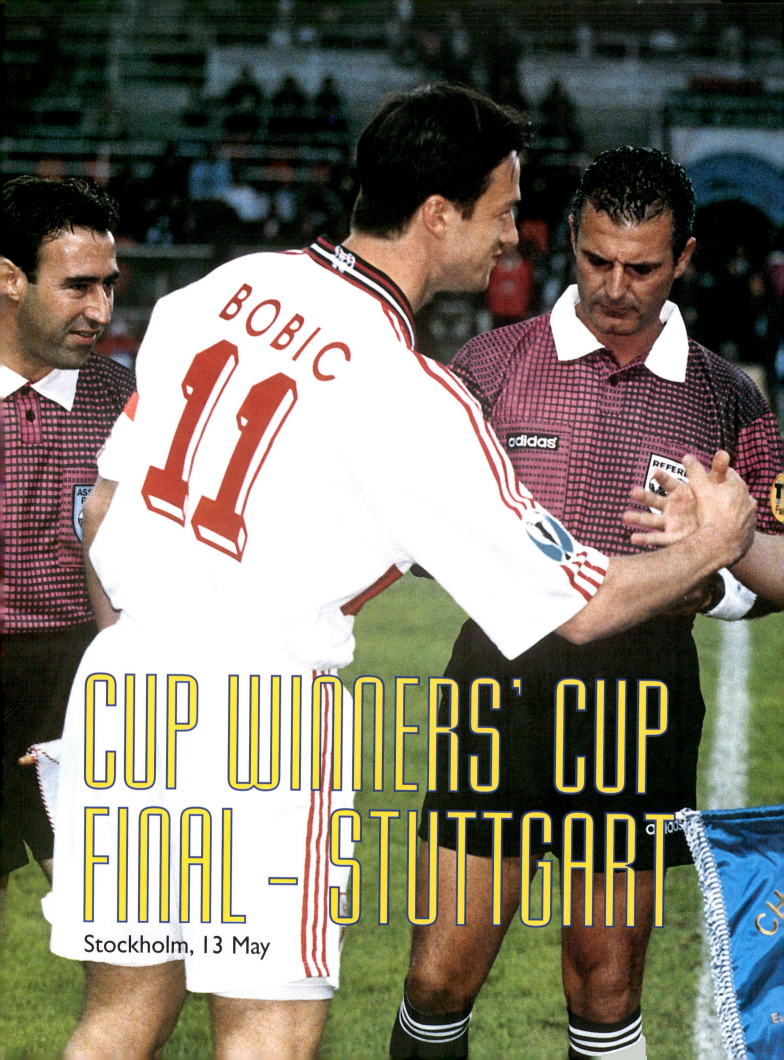

Chelsea's preparations for their most important game in the club's history were in turmoil almost before the celebrations after beating Vicenza had subsided. Dennis Wise received a dead leg in the second leg of the semi-final, Gianfranco Zola limped off in the opening minutes of the thrilling victory over Liverpool with a severe groin strain, Graeme Le Saux suffered a kick to the calf against Blackburn while Frank Sinclair had not played since the Coca-Cola Cup Final because of a calf strain. All these players were doubtful for the European final. Add the minor knocks to Dan Petrescu and Frank Leboeuf in the closing games of the domestic season and physios Mike Banks and Terry Byrne were under great pressure in the build up to the final.

At least Chelsea had no players suspended. Eight players, including the combative Dennis Wise, Gustavo Poyet, Michael

Duberry and Frank Leboeuf, had gone into the second leg of the semi-final against Vicenza knowing that a yellow card meant that they would miss the final. Fortunately the referee saw fit not to book any home players during the second leg even though the game had been played in such a competitive manner.

The victors of the other semi-final were not so lucky. Stuttgart's captain Frank Verlaat, and another defender Martin Spanring, were both cautioned for a second time in their second leg and would miss the showdown in Stockholm. The Germans appealed to UEFA to allow their captain to play. The governing body refused and Verlaat's absence from the final was to prove important.

The final weeks of the season were also clouded with controversy with regard to the last league fixture, at home against Bolton Wanderers, which was scheduled to take place only three days before Stockholm. Chelsea had asked the Premier League to move the game forward to help with preparations for the final but the League refused. Bolton were involved in the relegation fight and it was felt that it was unfair for all the clubs involved not to play their final fixture simultaneously. The Premier League even went so far as to issue a warning to Chelsea to field their strongest possible team against Bolton.

As it was, Roberto Di Matteo, Gianluca Vialli and Gustavo Poyet were named on the bench against Bolton and all three appeared for the second half. They replaced Dennis Wise, Tore Andre Flo and Dan Petrescu, three more internationals.

Chelsea defeated Bolton with late goals by Vialli and Morris to condemn Bolton to relegation.

The team flew out to Stockholm on the day before the fixture. Treatment for Zola and Le Saux continued until the last possible moment but it was clear that Sinclair would be unable to take part in the final.

Wise had come through his forty-five minutes against Bolton unscathed and he would captain the side. Zola trained on the morning of the final. There was no reaction to the groin strain but it was felt that he could not be risked for the entire ninety minutes. Vialli named himself to play alongside Flo in attack. The midfield quartet were to be the most

experienced players available, so the unlucky Eddie Newton missed out, while 23-year-old Danny Granville replaced Le Saux at left-back and so made only his third start in the competition just 14 months after signing from Third Division Cambridge United.

For Stuttgart Murat Yakin moved from midfield to replace Verlaat as sweeper. Otherwise they were at full strength with a very experienced line-up. Goalkeeper Franz Wohlfahrt, defender Thomas Berthold, midfielder Krassimir Balakov and striker Fredi Bobic were all well known to the Chelsea players. Stuttgart, like Chelsea, had finished the league season in fourth place and there was little to separate the two teams. Chelsea were confident though. They had the players that could score goals in any circumstances and they had proved over the two seasons they had been together that they could raise their game against any opponents. With the majority of the crowd on their side, they knew they could win.

The Rasunda Stadium, situated in Solna, a suburb to the north of Stockholm, is a compact ground with all four stands sited close to the pitch. When the two teams emerged on the pitch to the sound of the *Star Wars* theme around two-thirds of the 31,000 spectators were cheering Chelsea. In addition to those supporters who had purchased tickets through Chelsea's allocation, many fans had bought tickets from the stadium and were seated in the area reserved for neutrals. With Stuttgart returning all but 1,000 of their 12,000 allocation, the Chelsea players must have felt that they were stepping out to play a game at Stamford Bridge.

Chelsea looked to have settled the better, and in the opening minutes Di Matteo should have scored his third cup final goal when he dragged a shot wide after a clever pass by Poyet. Perhaps the rutted pitch, surely one of the worst to be used for a European final, had caused the

CUP WINNERS' CUP FINAL – STUTTGART

momentary hesitation in Di Matteo's mind before he shot. Stuttgart seemed to take heart from this let-off and began to dominate midfield. Without the cover normally supplied by Newton, the dangerous Bulgarian playmaker Balakov took over as the game's dominant force.

Chelsea's defence looked hesitant and a miscued clearance by Clarke fell for Bobic but he shot wide with a colleague unmarked in the penalty area. The best chance of the first half fell to Balakov. He burst from midfield past Clarke but could not find a way past the indomitable de Goey, who made a brilliant save low down just as the ball appeared to have sped past him into the net. It was yet another crucial intervention by the Dutchman who performed heroics throughout the cup campaigns.

Stuttgart were in control at this stage, but it proved to be the German team's best spell. Throughout the season, Chelsea had proved that they could raise their game at any stage and they did so again, creating chances almost at will. As the game moved towards the interval they went close on several occasions without ever looking certain to score. Flo battled well to place a header on the roof of the net, Poyet had a thunderous drive well parried by Wohlfahrt and Wise volleyed inches wide with the very last kick of the half.

At half-time, coach Graham Rix made the changes that would win the game for Chelsea. But they were minor alterations only as Chelsea were beginning to dominate the game. Di Matteo played rather more deeply than normal to compensate for the absence of Newton. Since moving to England, Di Matteo has made his name by getting forward and creating chances but here he sacrificed that part of his game to help eliminate the threat of Balakov. The tactic worked perfectly and allowed Wise the space to become the central figure of the game, giving yet another world-class performance.

Chelsea dominated possession in the second period, always pushing their opponents backwards. Still, they created few clear opportunities. Wise again shot narrowly wide, Granville produced an effort from the edge of the area that threatened to creep in until Wohlfahrt scrambled across and Vialli miscued a good chance.

Too often, the Chelsea attackers, particularly Flo, would do well to turn away from their marker only to be confronted by the spare man in defence. Berthold used all his experience to give an assured performance and ominously Stuttgart looked to have weathered the storm, even if their only clear chance came when the speedy Jonathan Akpoborie broke clear only for Granville to race back and get in a brilliant last ditch challenge.

Granville was the outstanding defender on the pitch, he was solid in the tackle, read the game well and grew in confidence sufficiently to get forward more often as the game went on. It was a masterly performance by the youngster that belied his lack of experience.

For all their control, Chelsea needed a cutting edge from somewhere and Rix turned to Gianfranco Zola. Last season's Football Writers' Footballer of the Year had endured a disappointing campaign. He had never fully recovered from a hamstring injury received shortly before the FA Cup Final and

his form had been patchy all season. A breathtaking display against Derby County in November saw him score three goals and it appeared as if his problems were behind him.

Sadly, Zola then went on a disastrous run. He didn't score again until March and he often looked short of confidence as doubts surfaced as to whether he would even make the Italian squad for the World Cup. It had seemed unthinkable a year ago that Zola could lose form this way. Goals against Real Betis and Vicenza saw the confidence come flooding back, but then disaster again struck with the groin strain suffered eighteen days before the final.

At that time it seemed certain that Zola would miss out not only on the World Cup but also the European Final. He spent the month in Rimini with the Italian masseuse Mimmo Pezza. The two-inch tear in the groin healed sufficiently for Zola to take his place on the substitute's bench if not to play from the start.

The frustrations of a disappointing season were blown away in the next 17 seconds. With his first touch, Zola controlled the ball and turned to face the defender. With his second, he was tackled. Zola's alert brain saw that the ball had broken to Wise and he continued forward. Wise played a precision pass to the edge of the area where Zola was now unmarked, the Stuttgart defenders having lost concentration for a split second following the substitution. As the ball bounced, Zola's third touch slammed it past the stranded goalkeeper into the roof of the goal.

20,000 Chelsea fans erupted in joy as the entire Chelsea team ran to congratulate Zola. On the bench, the first man to leap off in celebration was Flo, the man replaced by Zola and still putting his tracksuit top on. It was a wonderful moment that proved the collective spirit within the squad. In that moment, Stuttgart knew that they were a beaten team.

Eighteen minutes remained and Stuttgart did their best to move forward and snatch an equaliser but there was a lack of conviction about their efforts. Balakov hit a free-kick into the wall, they forced a couple of corners and hit two long-range shots over the bar, but even after Dan Petrescu was harshly sent off for a foul on Yakin with five minutes remaining, they failed to test de Goey seriously. The much maligned Chelsea

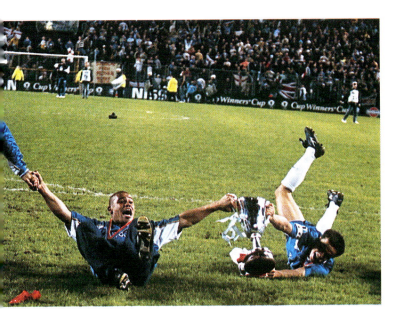

defence had now appeared in three cup finals in less than a year and kept clean sheets in all three.

Chelsea looked more threatening than their opponents, even when they were outnumbered. As Stuttgart made one last effort in injury time their goalkeeper ventured into the Chelsea half but he was stranded as the ball was cleared and Granville ran towards an empty net. The only Englishman to have scored in Chelsea's European campaign could have tried for a spectacular effort but instead chose wisely to run towards the corner before playing a deep cross that eventually was turned around for a corner. At least the youngster had used his head to use up a few more vital seconds. It was almost the last action of the game. Gerhard Poschner was sent off for dissent but it made no difference. The referee's whistle sounded immediately to give Chelsea their third major trophy within a year. After winning only four in the previous 91 years, these were riches indeed.

The celebrations were as spectacular as they had been at Wembley a year earlier. After they had collected the trophy, the players ran to all their supporters behind the goal in

which Zola had scored, before throwing themselves onto the turf. They then repeated the action at the other end. Vialli broke away from the melee to turn cartwheels along the touchline. Within three months of taking over from Gullit in controversial circumstances, he had become the first player-manager to lift a European trophy. After just 20 games, Vialli had become only the second Chelsea manager ever to lead the club to two trophies.

Finally, the players' last action before leaving the pitch was to kneel in the centre circle to say thank you to those supporters who a few years earlier could not have imagined being present on such an occasion.

For three days at least, Chelsea were the proud holders of three major trophies. The FA Cup, the Coca-Cola Cup and now the European Cup Winners' Cup had been won with a style and resolve that gave them the right to be regarded as the best cup team on the continent. At long last, Chelsea supporters could hail another great team: one that can now be regarded as the greatest ever Chelsea team and one that is determined that the adventure does not end here.